Lighten Up!

Book 2

Lighten Up!
Book 2
100 Funny Little Poems

Edited by Bruce Lansky

m Meadowbrook Press

Distributed by Simon & Schuster
New York

Library of Congress Cataloging-in-Publication Data
Lighten up! Book 2 / edited by Bruce Lansky.
        p.   cm.
    ISBN 0-671-31772-5 (Simon & Schuster)
    ISBN 0-88166-356-5 (Meadowbrook)
    1. Humorous poetry, American. I. Lansky, Bruce.
PS595.H8L59   1999
811'.0708—dc21   99-33561
                                                  CIP

Editor: Bruce Lansky
Coordinating Editor: Joseph Gredler
Production Manager: Joe Gagne
Production Assistant: Danielle White

© 1999 by Meadowbrook Creations

Cover photo: © TSM/Kunio Owaki, 96

Published by Meadowbrook Press, 5451 Smetana Drive, Minnetonka, Minnesota 55343

www.meadowbrookpress.com

BOOK TRADE DISTRIBUTION by Simon & Schuster, a division of Simon and Schuster, Inc., 1230 Avenue of the Americas, New York, NY 10020

03 02 01 00 99   10 9 8 7 6 5 4 3 2 1

Printed in the United States of America

Acknowledgments

We would like to thank the individuals who served
on reading panels for this project:

Susan D. Anderson, Kenneth L. Bastien, Mark Benthall,
Dorothy Brummel, Maureen Cannon, Gail Clark, Faye W.
Click, William Rossa Cole, Edmund Conti, Pat D'Amico,
Doug Dosson, Gene Fehler, Charles L. Grove, Babs Bell
Hajdusiewicz, Dick Hayman, Henry Hill, Paul Humphrey,
Jo S. Kittinger, Sydnie Meltzer Kleinhenz, Helen Ksypka,
Joyce LaMers, Felicia Lamport, Irene Livingston, Cynthia
MacGregor, Fay Whitman Manus, Jean Marvin, Bob McKenty,
Charlene Meltzer, Lois Muehl, Ned Pastor, Marcy S. Powell,
Mae Scanlan, Lawrence Schimel, Rita Schlachter, Rosemary
Schmidt, Robert Scotellaro, Sherri Shunfenthal,
Denise Tiffany, Timothy Tocher, Evelyn Amuedo Wade,
Margaret Woodall

Table of Contents

Food and Drink

Domestic Tranquility

Every time I try to shake the ketchup out of a ketchup bottle, the words to Richard Armour's famous poem on page 21 pop into my head. And when I'm visiting New York wondering whether to walk or take a cab through Central Park, Ogden Nash's "City Greenery" on page 44 comes to mind.

Most of the poems in this book are like that: They'll pop into your mind whenever a particular topic arises, because they package a witty observation in a highly memorable form.

Do you have to make a speech? Check out the advice in "Before You Make a Speech" on page 68. Is there a family reunion on your calendar? Before you do anything drastic, consult Charles Ghigna's "Family Reunion" on page 29. Have you been asked by a doctor or "loved ones" to cut back on your consumption of alcohol? You might enjoy "Liquor and Longevity" on page 93. Does your wife give you grief about leaving the toilet seat up? Browse Bob McKenty's "Ode de Toilette" on page 8.

If you've taken the time to read any of the above poems, you've discovered a few things:

1) It's almost impossible to read just one.
2) It's almost impossible to read one without smiling.
3) It's almost impossible to read one without sharing it.

That's pretty much what happens to me every time I read the poems in this book—which is why I'm now sharing them with you.

Bruce Lansky

Joyce Kilmer Recites
at Barnes and Noble

I think that I shall never see
—Polly, pick up on line 3.
A poem lovely as a tree.

A tree whose hungry mouth is pressed
—Fire drill! (It's just a test.)
Against the earth's sweet flowing breast;

A tree that looks at God all day
—Patronize our new café.
And lifts her leafy arms to pray;

A tree that may in summer wear
—Price check, Chuck, on *Truth or Dare*.
A nest of robins in her hair;

Upon whose bosom snow has lain;
—Fred in Fiction: find Mark Twain.
Who intimately lives with the rain.

Poems are made by fools like me,
—Closing time. Leave quietly.

—Bob McKenty

The Way to my Heart

You baked me a cake in the shape of a heart.
I eagerly ate it, thus doing my part.
The way to my heart is my stomach, it's true—
And both are much bigger today, thanks to you.

—Bob McKenty

The Peacemaker

My wife and I have arguments,
But they don't last for long.
In fact, they're over just as soon
As I admit I'm wrong.

—*Richard Armour*

The Road Less Traveled

My marriage has unraveled
Because of Robert Frost.
When I take the road less traveled
My wife insists I'm lost.

—Bob McKenty

Compromise

In wines my wife prefers the red,
While I like white the best.
And so we drink rosé instead,
Which both of us detest.

—*Graal Braun*

Liver Lovers

My wife cooks liver once a week
and serves it lightly peppered;
I always sneak it off my plate
to feed our German shepherd.

My wife cooks liver once a week;
she says it's very nourishing;
I guess she must be right because
our German shepherd's flourishing.

—*Leslie Danford Perkins*

Taking Her Pick

My wife possessively asserts
Her wifely right to pick my shirts.
With steady hands and birdlike eyes
She picks my hats and socks and ties.
She picks, like other wives and mamas,
My underwear and my pajamas.
She picks my coats, both sport and top,
And there I'd let the matter drop,
Except as I observe with rue,
She sometimes picks my pockets too.

—*Richard Armour*

In House Critic

I always buy clothes
With my wife on the spot
To let me know whether
I like them or not.

—Henry Hill

Ode de Toilette

The medicine chest harbors *eau de toilette,*
Dozens of bobby pins and a barrette,
Several lipsticks in several shades,
Squeezers and tweezers and her razor blades,
Scattered assortments of rouges and blushes,
Powders to temper the consequent flushes,
Herbal shampoos and some mousses and gels—
A Secret compartment for colors and smells
With nary a nook for his small shaving cup.
How *dare* she complain when the toilet seat's up!

—Bob McKenty

Room Service

Breakfast in bed, being pampered and petted,
　　You'll have to admit is quite slick.
There's only one trouble: in *our* house, to get it
　　You'll have to be terribly sick.

—Richard Armour

His mother's eyes,
His father's chin,
His auntie's nose,
His uncle's grin,

His great-aunt's hair,
His grandma's ears,
His grandpa's mouth,
So it appears...

Poor little tot,
Well may he moan.
He hasn't much
To call his own.

—*Richard Armour*

Revolution

What time I spend with colored threads
replacing buttons Junior sheds!
And while I sew, I often rave
about the time that I could save
if children's buttons only grew
in neatly packaged sets of two,
with new ones ready underneath
to pop in place like second teeth.

—*Evelyn Amuedo Wade*

Mind Your Manners, Kids

Don't drum on the table.
Don't play with your food.
Don't talk while you're chewing;
It's terribly rude.

Don't leave the fridge open.
Don't slam the screen door.
Don't throw dirty laundry
all over the floor.

Don't fight with your brother.
Don't pull the cat's tail.
Don't open your big sister's
personal mail.

Don't pester your parents.
Don't stick out your tongue.
Don't do what your parents did
when they were young.

—Bruce Lansky

Double Duty

Mothers who raise
A child by the book
Can, if sufficiently vexed,
Hasten results
By applying the book
As well as applying the text.

—*W. E. Farbstein*

Transportation Problem

Kiddy cars of little tikes,
Slightly older children's bikes,
Skis and sleds for winter needs,
Wagons, trucks, velocipedes,
Scooters, ice (and roller) skates—
How the stuff accumulates—
Piles of articles vehicular,
On the front porch in particular,
Things your children go like heck on,
And you fall and break your neck on.

—*Richard Armour*

Memo to a Camp Director

You have, beneath your muscled wing,
Our three beloved sons.
You also have their hamster pets,
Their rockets, ropes, and guns.
You have our whole vacation fund
To meet your fancy fee.
And, sportsmanlike, I must admit
You have our sympathy.

—*Alma Denny*

Driving Lesson

I taught my daughter how to drive,
She finally got it right;
She goes on green and stops on red—
And brakes when I turn white.

—*Charles Ghigna*

A Grandchild Is the Greatest Joy

A grandchild is the greatest joy
That anyone can know—
A sweet, cherubic girl or boy
Who'll grow and grow and grow
Into another problem child
(watch history repeat)
Who'll drive your son or daughter wild.
You bet revenge is sweet!

—*Bob McKenty*

Perilous Fight

O say, can you see by the dawn's early light?
Till after my third cup of coffee, not quite.

—*Bob McKenty*

Wine Coolers

No cork to eye, no sniff, no sip,
No inner fear that you might slip;
No vintage year, no strained pretense,
No sneering sommelier to fence;
No predrink ritual or puzzle—
Just open, pour, and start to guzzle!

—*Bern Sharfman*

Growing Pains

We're growing tomatoes,
A high yielding plant.
We eat what we can
And can what we can't.

—*Henry Hill*

Shake and shake
The catsup bottle,
None will come,
And then a lot'll.

—*Richard Armour*

Eggplant

This purple orb upon a stem
Seems much less food than bright décor,
A giant semiprecious gem,
An egg laid by some dinosaur.
In France the eggplant first was tried
At banquets of the Sun King, Louis.
It tastes quite good if crisply fried,
But better yet in ratatouille.

—*Ross P. Steel*

The Sweetbread

That sweetbread gazing up at me
Is not what it purports to be.
Says Webster in one paragraph,
It is the pancreas of a calf.
Since it is neither sweet nor bread,
I think I'll take a bun instead.

—Ogden Nash

Guests

Some cause happiness with their smiles,
Some by being deft,
Some by being right on time,
Some by having left.

—*Charles Lee*

Week-End Flotsam

My week-end guests who leave behind
The articles I later find
(The toothbrush and the glasses case,
The hat, the garment trimmed with lace,
The camera, the overshoes,
The bathrobe, bright in many hues)
Should also leave, just as unfailing,
A little cash to cover mailing.

—*Richard Armour*

Instructions to an Overnight Guest

Before you go to bed, dear guest,
Before you close your eyes in rest,
Please let me take you, first, in tow,
And teach you what you need to know.

Here is a door that will not lock—
You keep it shut with this small rock.
These drawers stick—just grip them tightly
And lift them up, while twisting slightly.
Beware this light switch—do not touch;
Unscrew the bulb, but not too much.

This clock gains half an hour each night;
Subtract the same to tell time right.
I think I also should explain
The tub is rather slow to drain,
And if this faucet drips, you'll find
The cutoff valve (and wrench) behind.

Before you come again, we'll mend
The faucet, drawers, and switch, my friend;
The door, the drain, the half-hour-fast time—
Or did I tell you this the last time?

—*Richard Armour*

A Man for All Seasonings

"Pass the salt," I say and yet
Salt and pepper's what I get.
If "Pass the pepper" I should yell,
Salt would come along as well.
Like man and wife, like sister, brother,
Where the one is, there's the other.
Though salt has many times the takers,
Pepper's in as many shakers.
So don't object, and don't be loath—
Just ask for one, accept them both.

—Richard Armour

Family Reunion

We used to gather once a year,
We all were quite a clan;
Now, I miss those gatherings—
As often as I can.

—Charles Ghigna

A Hex on My Neighbor's Green Thumb

May your shovel break, may your fertilizer bake,
May your droughts be long and dusty.
May moles make holes, may blights take tolls,
May your pruning tools get rusty.
A killing frost on the hybrids you crossed,
May your pink chrysanthemums sicken.
A pox on your phlox, may your seeds fall on rocks,
May your aphids and mealy-bugs thicken.
And to add to your woes, may you slice up your hose
When you run your power mower.
One last incantation: While you're on vacation
May stinkweed grow up to your door.
At the next Garden Show they'll surely know
Just who should have gotten first prize.
My brow with sweat was twice as wet,
And twice as green were my eyes!

—*Glenna Holloway*

The Driveway Needs Sealing

The driveway needs sealing;
The lawn mower's busted;
The wallpaper's peeling;
The railing is rusted;
The windows need stripping;
The chair legs need glue;
The faucets are dripping
(The gutters are too);
The fireplace needs bricks. It
Has gone bad to worse.
And where's Mr. Fixit?
He's writing this verse.

—Bob McKenty

The Three Seasons

There are only three seasons
That homeowners know:
And they are called rake
And shovel and mow.

—*Pat D'Amico*

Fall Guy

I study the leaves
And consider the fall of them.
Shall I rake up piecemeal
Or wait till there's all of them?

My wife says the first
Would be neater. No matter.
As I lean on my rake
I lean more to the latter.

—*Richard Armour*

The Bachelor

The bachelor's a useful man,
Be sure to know one if you can.
He's fine to ask to dinner when
You're just a little short of men.
And when he comes, this chap so handy,
He brings a two-pound box of candy
And, dinner done, this helpful type
Stays willingly to wash or wipe.
A playful chap, devoid of pomp,
He takes the children for a romp
And tells them tales and, having fed them,
Considers it a lark to bed them.
But here's the puzzling paradox:
Instead of locking all the locks
And pulling shades and barring doors
And keeping him to do her chores,
The hostess cannot wait to choose him
A darling wife, and promptly lose him.

—Richard Armour

Give Me This Day...

My wants and needs are simple
a little house that's cozy,
a tree to shade my garden swing,
a sunset, wide and rosy,

sweet peace throughout the planet,
and friendship, warm and funny,
and two more teensy, weensy things:
FANTASTIC SEX AND MONEY!!!

—*Irene Livingston*

And So Too Bad

I dearly love to read in bed
And while I read to munch on bread
With cheese or liverwurst or ham
Or peanut butter mixed with jam.

Yes, while I read, I sandwich in
Some sandwiches, and wipe my chin
If mayonnaise perchance should drip
Beyond my guarding lower lip.

Caught by a story, ere I stop
A bit of this or that I drop
And know by feel, or light of dawn,
Which side my bed is buttered on.

—Richard Armour

Sheep That Pass in the Night

It's often said that counting sheep
Will help a person fall asleep.
Attempting to resolve my doubt
About this scheme, I tried it out
And did my utmost to assign
Each sheep its tally in the line.
I muffed it, which was hard to take.
I simply couldn't stay awake
To count a fairly decent number.
I foundered, comatose in slumber.

—*Irene Warsaw*

In a Lather

One of the things I've tried quite hard,
    But still haven't managed to cope with,
Is the cake of soap that's too thick to discard,
    But a little too thin to soap with.

—*Richard Armour*

Bathtub Complaint

No singer in bathtubs, I lift up my voice
Against a contraption that gives me the choice
Of sitting bolt upright and warming my knees
While my chest and my back and my upper parts freeze,
Or dunking the top of me, fore part and aft,
And exposing my legs and my feet to the draft.
In short, I'm too long, and I can't for the soul of me
Submerge, as I'd like, at one moment the whole of me.
So I shift back and forth and unhappily fidget
And swear that the tub was designed by a midget.

—*Richard Armour*

Limerick

I finished a sculpture today.
I made it from soup tins and clay.
I put it outside
to show off with pride,
but the garbage men took it away.

—*Norma Dixon*

My Country 'Tis of Thee

Waste disposal
Nowadays seems
To attract promoters
Of fraudulent schemes.
How did it happen
That we've come to be
The home of the knave
And the land of debris?

—Henry Hill

Plate-Glass Doors

Plate-glass doors form a dangerous duo:
Never, when using them, try
To enter the place by the one marked TUO
Or withdraw through the one marked NI.

—*Roy Fuller*

Is My Face Red!

Imagine you've shopped
in a posh little store.
You start to depart
through the wide-open door

when *crash* goes your forehead!
The glass door was closed.
It's not standing open,
the way you supposed.

You grin; you feel foolish.
The door was too clean:
All glass should be dirty
enough to be seen!

—*Irene Livingston*

City Greenery

If you should happen after dark
To find yourself in Central Park,
Ignore the paths that beckon you
And hurry, hurry to the zoo,
And creep into the tiger's lair.
Frankly, you'll be safer there.

—*Ogden Nash*

Trees

I think that I shall never ski
On any slope that has a tree
That waits in ambush night and day
Extending lethal limbs to prey,
A tree whose knotty trunk is scarred
From scores of skiers who hit it hard.
A tree that stands upon the slopes
Where patiently it waits and hopes
For skulls to crush or bones to crack
Of one who's wandered off the track.
(Poems are made by wimps like me
Who haven't got the guts to ski.)

—*Bob McKenty*

Holding Patter

I like mellow music;
I relish the news;
A market report
Or some movie reviews.
But when I'm on hold
I am often appalled
To find I've forgotten
The reason I called.

—*Pat D'Amico*

Bad Hair Day

I went to my barber
and sat in his chair.
I asked him politely
to cut off some hair.

I must have dozed off
when he started to cut.
When I woke up my head
was as bald as my butt.

When you go to the barber
do not take a nap.
Or, like me, you'll be hiding
your head in a cap.

—*Bruce Lansky*

Just One Thing...

My car is looking
Showroom clean.
They've just rebuilt
The whole machine
And I hope
Before they're done
They'll find out why
It doesn't run.

—Henry Hill

Bend in the Road

The road map tells us where to go
and how to go and when;
too bad it doesn't tell us how
to fold it up again.

—*Charles Ghigna*

How Drivers Communicate

You can indicate directions
with the blinkers in your car.
You can honk your horn if someone
doesn't notice where you are.

You can wave a little "thank you"
when a driver lets you go.
In emergencies your flashers
or a flare is apropos.

But of all the many signals,
there is one that seems to linger.
It's the universal message
when you raise your middle finger.

—*Helen Ksypka*

Traffic Rule I

One traffic rule
we all obey:
*the Mack truck has
the right of way.*

—*N. M. Bodecker*

We're Careful about That

We're sorry to tell you
There'll be some delay.
Your flight will depart
Sometime later today.

We'll give you the time
As soon as we get it
And all of us here
Sincerely regret it.

We'll tell you as soon
As we know when and where.
We never leave passengers
Up in the air.

—Henry Hill

What I Think about When Traveling

When strapped into an airplane seat,
I wonder where to put my feet.

And as the plane soars through the sky,
I wonder how the thing can fly.

And when I use the airplane john,
I wonder who it's flushing on.

And when we're finally on the ground,
I wonder where my bags are bound.

And when I'm in the parking lot,
I wonder why my car is not.

—*Bruce Lansky*

Risky Business

I see a stock,
I think I'll try it,
Down it goes
After I buy it.
What gets me down
Is why the hell it
Goes right up
After I sell it!

—*Fay Whitman Manus*

Reading Matters

Before you invest
Always read the prospectus.
It's required by laws
Designed to protect us.
Buried somewhere therein
Under mountains of prose
Are all of the risks that
They're forced to expose.
Don't know where to start?
Let me give you a hint:
The greater the hazards
The smaller the print.

—*Henry Hill*

Coin Return

Although I try, I cannot spurn
The place on phones marked "Coin Return."
A strange compulsion makes me linger
And test with probing index finger.

Let me but say to those not bound
By such a habit: I have found
That this exploratory itch
Is not a way of getting rich.

—*Richard Armour*

Trip Tip

When packing for a trip abroad,
I know this may sound funny:
pack half the clothes you think you need—
and twice as much the money.

—*Charles Ghigna*

In the Beginning

As I've learned at the cost of many a buck
    Since my days as a starry-eyed lad,
There *is* such a thing as "beginner's luck,"
    And more often than not, it's bad.

—*Richard Armour*

Reality Checks

The facts of life come to us all,
Arriving unannounced;
Reality's the only check
That no one ever bounced.

—Charles Ghigna

The Irony of Being Different

The rebels of the world we see
    Define their eccentricity
By wearing clothes and styling hair
    Designed to make us stop and stare.
The irony in what they do
    Is many others will then too
Appear in this outlandish way,
    And we'll be odd instead of they.

—*Richard Vaules, Jr.*

Who, Me? Bigoted?

One thing I simply can't abide—
    (Forgive me my restrictions)
Is finding someone whom I loathe,
    Who shares my deep convictions.

—*Evelyn Amuedo Wade*

Anatomically Speaking

I'm wary of putting my foot in my mouth,
and shaking a leg just fatigues me;
Whenever I dare to stick my neck out,
the consequence never intrigues me.
I can't seem to keep a stiff upper lip,
and my eye for detail's rather weak;
Now you know why I play it by ear,
and converse with my tongue in my cheek.

—*Ned Pastor*

Metaphorically Speaking

She's one cookie short of a dozen.
There aren't many peas in her pod.
Her fence doesn't have all its pickets.
Her curtain is missing a rod.
She's got too few bristles to brush with.
The handle won't fit in her door.
There's nothing quite like a good putdown
Expressed in a quaint metaphor.

—*Jill Williams*

Asian Flu

Miserable flu—
The ache, the chill, the fever…
The sneeze…ah…hai-KU!

—*C. L. Grove*

O I C

I'm in a 10der mood 2day
& feel poetic, 2;
4 fun I'll just — off a line
& send it off 2 U.

I'm sorry you've been 6 so long;
Don't B disconsol8;
But bear your ills with 42de,
& they won't seem so gr8.

—*Anonymous*

On Using My First Computer

No more will I retype a page
to change a single line;
though erring may be human,
deleting is divine.

—*Leslie Danford Perkins*

Ode to the Spell Checker

Eye halve a spelling chequer
It came with my pea sea
It plainly marques four my revue
Miss steaks eye kin knot sea.

Eye strike a key and type a word
And weight four it two say
Weather eye am wrong oar write
It shows me strait a weigh.
As soon as a mist ache is maid
It nose bee fore two long
And eye can put the error rite
Its rare lea ever wrong.

Eye have run this poem threw it
I am shore your pleased two no
Its letter perfect awl the weigh
My chequer tolled me sew.

—Anon A. Mouse

Before You Make a Speech

Don't be nervous.
Don't be shy.
Clear your throat.
Straighten your tie.

Look your audience
in the eye.
Then smile with confidence
as you zip up your fly.

—*Bruce Lansky*

It Goes without Saying

To say, "Needless to say,"
    is a needless concession,
For if it's not needed,
    why use the expression?

If the phrase is not needed
    (this thought to convey)
Then it's needless to say
    that it's needless to say.

—*Mark Burds*

Inscription for a Fly Swatter

The hand is quicker than the eye is,
But somewhat slower than the fly is.

—*Richard Armour*

The Termite

Some primal termite knocked on wood
And tasted it, and found it good,
And that is why your Cousin May
Fell through the parlor floor today.

—*Ogden Nash*

The Shark

The shark's a live torpedo,
Slipping silent through the sea.
Its warhead is its gaping jaws;
Its target might be—me!

So when I swim in coastal waters,
Usually I try
To stay in crowds of bathers more
delectable than I.

—*C. L. Grove*

The Shark

How many Scientists have written
The shark is gentle as a kitten!
Yet this I know about the shark:
His bite is worser than his bark.

—*Ogden Nash*

Shaggy-Dog Story

He has to be trained,
He has to be fed,
He has to be washed,
He has to be led.

He has to be combed
And worked on with shears,
He has to have cockleburs
Plucked from his ears.

"Look out for the dog,"
The sign on our door,
Isn't meant as a warning,
It's meant as a chore.

—*Richard Armour*

My Little Dog

Where oh where has my little dog gone?
Right in the middle of my neighbor's lawn.

—*Tonita S. Gardner*

The Turtle

The turtle lives 'twixt plated decks
Which practically conceal its sex.
I think it clever of the turtle
In such a fix to be so fertile.

—*Ogden Nash*

They Multiplied

Noah, not knowing their habits,
Started his trip with two rabbits.
Without him, there wouldn't be any.
But, now, there are far, far too many.

—*Bruce Lansky*

Hippopotamus

Who could love you,
Hippopotamus?

You're gross, you're rude, you're...
Likealotofus!

—C. L. Grove

The Aardvark

The aardvark is, to say the least,
A seldom seen or heard of beast,

And yet a certain sort of fame
Attaches to this creature's name,

For with its double-barrelled a's
In proud pre-eminence it stays

Year after year up at the very
Beginning of the dictionary.

—*Richard Armour*

The Ostrich

The ostrich roams the great Sahara.
Its mouth is wide, its neck is narra.
It has such long and lofty legs,
I'm glad it sits to lay its eggs.

—*Ogden Nash*

The Codfish

The codfish lays 10,000 eggs,
The homely hen just one;
The codfish never cackles
To tell you that she's done.
And so we scorn the codfish,
And the homely hen we prize.
Which demonstrates to you and me
That it pays to advertise.

—*Anonymous*

Wash Out

Two beavers in a mountain rill
    Decided as they swam:
The little stream was cute, but still
    It wasn't worth a dam.

—*Paul Humphrey*

Good-bye, Goldfish

The day my favorite goldfish died,
I'm not ashamed to say, I cried.
I prayed for its departed soul,
then flushed it down the toilet bowl.

—*Bruce Lansky*

Lunch Crunch

We grab a salad on the run,
No time to sit and chat;
We hunger for those good old days
When we could chew the fat.

—*Charles Ghigna*

Georgy Porgy

Georgy Porgy, pudding and pie,
I'll bet your cholesterol's way too high.

—Tonita S. Gardner

A Losing Battle

MacArthur, Bradley, Patton—though
you triumphed with your troops,
you never met the enemy
of ice cream (triple scoops).

You never fought a craving for
a butter-frosted cake;
you never had to strategize
against a chocolate shake.

You never were surrounded by
a bowl of crunchy chips
or ambushed by an apple pie
or tangy, tasty dips.

To decorated gen'rals, I
respectfully divulge,
you, too, would be a loser in
the battle of the bulge.

—Helen Ksypka

Let Us Spray

A joy of which I'll not partake
Is eating children's birthday cake.
The milestones that they celebrate
Inspire kids to salivate.
To "blow out" candles, in a word,
Is really patently absurd:
Each puff contains sufficient moisture
To cultivate your av'rage oyster.
So, birthday-boy and ditto-daughter,
Withhold from me your whiff of water.
I do not need some little squirt
To atomize on my dessert.
Among the things I cannot do
Is have my cake and drink it too.

—Robert G. Wombacher

The Cold Facts

"Virus" is a Latin word
That doctors won't define
Because they know the meaning is
"Your guess is good as mine."

—*Charles Ghigna*

Where It Hurts the Most

When it comes to dentists,
People hate to go.
They fear the pain, the Novocain,
For me, that isn't so.
It seems that I can tolerate
The needles and the drill,
But I can't stand the pain I get,
When I receive the bill!

—*Fay Whitman Manus*

Hair Lines

My wife complains about her hair,
but she has no excuse;
for hers is only turning gray
while mine is turning loose.

—*Charles Ghigna*

Middle Age

Middle age
Is a time of life
That a man first notices
In his wife.

—*Richard Armour*

Blow Hard

Another candle on your cake?
Well, that's no cause to pout.
Be glad that you have strength enough
to blow the damn thing out.

—*William R. Evans III and
    Andrew Frothingham*

Liquor and Longevity

The horse and mule live 30 years
And nothing know of wine and beers.
The goat and sheep at 20 die.
And never taste of Scotch or Rye.
The cow drinks water by the ton
And at 18 is mostly done.
The dog at 15 cashes in
Without the aid of rum and gin.
The cat in milk and water soaks
And then in 12 short years it croaks.
The modest, sober, bone-dry hen
Lays eggs for nogs, then dies at ten.
All animals are strictly dry:
They sinless live and swiftly die;
But sinful, ginful rum-soaked men
Survive for three score years and ten.
And some of them, a very few,
Stay pickled till they're 92.

—Anonymous

Typical Optical

In the days of my youth
    'Mid many a caper
I drew with my nose
    A mere inch from the paper;
But now that I'm older
    And of the elite
I find I can't focus
    inside of two feet.

First pill-bottle labels
    And telephone books
Began to go under
    To my dirty looks;
Then want-ads and box scores
    Succumbed to the plague
Of the bafflingly quite
    Unresolvably vague.

Old novels and poems
    By Proust and John Donne
Recede from my ken in
    Their eight-point Granjon;
Long, long in the lens
    My old eyeballs enfold
No print any finer
    Than sans-serif **bold.**

—John Updike

General Custer

General Custer rode with pride.
The lust for battle filled him.
Hell-bent was he on Siouxicide
And—sure enough—it killed him!

—*Bob McKenty*

The Purist

I give you now Professor Twist,
A conscientious scientist,
Trustees exclaimed, "He never bungles!"
And sent him off to distant jungles.
Camped on a tropic riverside,
One day he missed his loving bride.
She had, the guide informed him later,
Been eaten by an alligator.
Professor Twist could not but smile.
"You mean," he said, "a crocodile."

—*Ogden Nash*

Mike O'Day

This is the grave of Mike O'Day
Who died maintaining his right of way.
His right was clear, his will was strong,
But he's just as dead as if he'd been wrong.

—*Anonymous*

Passport to Paradise

He passed a car without a fuss.
He passed a cart of hay.
He tried to pass a swerving bus,
And then he passed away.

—*Anonymous*

Lead Kindly Light

Where Bishop Patrick crossed the street
An "X" now marks the spot.
The light of God was with him,
But the traffic light was not.

—*E. Y. Harburg*

To a Human Skeleton

It's hard to think,
Albeit true,
That without flesh
I'd be like you,

And harder still
To think, old pal,
That one of these
Fine days I shall.

—Richard Armour

Author Index

Title Index

106

Credits

107

Other Titles Edited by Bruce Lansky

Humor books:

Age Happens
Familiarity Breeds Children
For Better And For Worse
Golf: It's Just a Game!
Lovesick
Work and Other Occupational Hazards

Adult poetry books:

Lighten Up!

Children's poetry books:

A Bad Case of the Giggles
Happy Birthday to Me!
Kids Pick the Funniest Poems
Miles of Smiles
No More Homework! No More Tests!
Poetry Party

To order a book or catalog call toll-free: 800-338-2232
or visit our website: www.meadowbrookpress.com